Lech Walesa

Lech Walesa

Caroline Lazo

Peacemakers

DILLON PRESS
New York

Maxwell Macmillan Canada
Toronto

Maxwell Macmillan International
New York Oxford Singapore Sydney

To Jean

Acknowledgments

Special thanks to Peter Lazo for his research assistance

Photo Credits

All photos courtesy of AP—Wide World Photos

Book design by Carol Matsuyama

Library of Congress Cataloging-in-Publication Data

Lazo, Caroline Evensen.
    Lech Walesa / by Caroline Lazo. — 1st ed.
        p. cm. — (Peacemakers)
    Includes bibliographical references and index.
        Summary: A biography of the Polish union organizer who became his country's first elected president in 1990.
    ISBN 0-87518-525-8
        1. Walesa, Lech, 1943- —Juvenile literature. 2. Presidents—Poland—Biography—Juvenile literature. [1. Walesa, Lech, 1943- . 2. Presidents—Poland. 3. Labor unions—Biography.] I Title. II. Series.
    DK4452.W34L39   1993
    943.805'6'092—dc20
    [B]   92-39959

Dillon Press   Maxwell Macmillan Canada, Inc.
Macmillan Publishing Company   1200 Eglinton Avenue East
866 Third Avenue   Suite 200
New York, NY 10022   Don Mills, Ontario M3C 3N1

Macmillan Publishing Company is part of the Maxwell Communication Group of Companies.

First Edition

Printed in the United States of America

10 9 8 7 6 5 4 3 2 1

Epigraph

We shall not yield to violence. We shall not be deprived of union freedoms . . . and persons sentenced for defending union and civic rights must be set free. The defense of our rights and our dignity, as well as efforts never to let ourselves be overcome by the feeling of hatred—this is the road we have chosen.

—*Lech Walesa*

Russian president Boris Yeltsin welcomes Lech Walesa during talks at the Kremlin regarding the removal of Russian troops from Poland.

Contents

Lech Walesa addresses a crowd of striking workers.

Introduction

Sometimes a single foul-up—like missing a train—can change the course of a man's life and lead him into positions of power he never dreamed of before.

In 1967 Lech Walesa (pronounced *Valensa*), an unemployed electrician, took a train bound for Gdynia, Poland, where he hoped to find a job. On the way the train stopped in Gdansk long enough for passengers to leave their seats and visit the station before boarding again. But Lech, then 24 years old, lost track of the time as he listened to local workers discussing jobs in Poland, and the train left for Gdynia without him.

Restless and not sure what to do next, he walked outside the station, where he ran into an old friend, who urged him to stay in Gdansk and apply for work there. Lech had nothing to lose, so he stayed. He applied at the Lenin Shipyard, where he got a job as a naval electrician.

Three years later, he helped lead his fellow workers in the first mass protest against a Communist government. Skyrocketing food prices had led to the strike, but when the peaceful protest turned into a riot, Walesa saw four of his friends, unarmed, killed by their own country's soldiers . . . and he would never forget it. He made a commitment to continue the struggle for fair food prices, decent wages, and the natural right to live in peace. Even if it took a lifetime to achieve, Walesa would never waver from his goal.

Between 1970 and 1980, workers' strikes made history in Poland because, until Walesa organized one, such actions were unheard of there. Like Gandhi, Walesa believed in nonviolence—and was jailed for inspiring people to protest unfair laws. Though his labor organization, Solidarity, was stripped of its rights and forced underground in Poland, Walesa won praise around the world, and in 1983 received the Nobel Peace Prize.

Like Gandhi, Walesa and his ten million followers refused to give up their nonviolent fight for human rights. In 1989, when the Polish leaders needed Walesa's help (his organizational skills and expertise), Solidarity was relegalized. And the following year, in the first free election in his country's history, Lech Walesa became the president of Poland.

The story of Lech Walesa is also a story of family love, respect, hard work, and good humor—especially in school. "It isn't really good to be too gifted," he wrote in his memoirs. "I prefer to be like the bee, which knows it is perfectly able to collect honey, but which doesn't rush headlong for the big beehive, where it could fall in and get stuck."

But it was Walesa's commitment to peace through nonviolence that brought freedom to Poland and endeared him to the world. "I'm a man who believes in dialogue and agreement," he wrote. "We have already tried and tested every form of violence, and not once in the entire course of human history has anything good or lasting come from it."

Lech Walesa passes a mural of Holocaust prisoners during a tour of the Yad Vashem Holocaust Memorial in Jerusalem.

12

Rediscovering Poland

Both beauty and terror haunt the history of Poland. Frédéric Chopin, Adam Mickiewicz, Czeslaw Milosz, Andrzei Wajda, and Henryk Sienkiewicz are just a few of the artists whose music, poetry, films, and novels symbolize the beauty and creative power that flow from the small country. At the same time, the name *Auschwitz* recalls the horror that held Poland in its grip during Adolf Hitler's reign of terror. Six million innocent Poles—including three million Jews—were tortured and killed in death camps like Auschwitz during World War II.

When the Soviet Union and its allies finally conquered Hitler's armies and won World War II, Poles saw a chance for peace in their war-torn country. But their hopes were dashed as the Soviet-controlled Communist party inflicted its own kind of terror, in the form of censorship, harassment of church activities, and imprisonment of those who opposed the Communist doctrine.

Still, brave Poles would persevere and refuse to give up hope for a rebirth of justice in their beloved country. After all, Poland had once been the most democratic country in Europe!

In the 17th century most of Europe was ruled by kings whose right to govern, they believed, came from God and was undisputed. But in Poland the king's power came from the aristocracy, who elected him and put limits on his rule. Afraid that he might gain too much power, the nobility refused to give their king a standing army. As a result, Poland grew vulnerable, and by the end of the 18th century was swallowed up by surrounding nations.

During World War I, when those nations became embroiled in their own battles, the Poles formed the underground Polish Military Organization in the hope of setting themselves free from the "partition powers" (Germany, Austria, Hungary, and Russia) that ruled them. And when the Allies (France, Great Britain, and the United States) finally won that war, Poland won its independence. Throughout those troubled times Poles kept their identity alive through their loyalty to one another, to their church (mainly Catholic), and to a perseverance that, later, both Hitler and Stalin would try— but fail—to crush.

Sandwiched between Germany and the Soviet Union,

Poland continued to be preyed upon by its powerful neighbors. Though it regained its independence after World War I, it lost it when Hitler invaded Poland in 1939, and again when Joseph Stalin's Soviet forces ousted the Nazis at the end of World War II.

By 1948 the Polish United Workers party (PZPR), founded by the Soviet Union, was established in Poland, and by 1953 Soviet-dictated communism was firmly in place there. The PZPR selected certain party members to direct all of Poland's institutions. But communism in Poland was not as harsh as in the rest of Eastern Europe or in the Soviet Union itself, where churches were closed and all farms were state-owned. Though Polish churches were regarded as "counterrevolutionary," they still stayed open. And while most of a farmer's income had to be turned over to the state, most farms remained privately owned, including the Walesas' small farm in north-central Poland.

But the constant and terrible violations of human rights—the arrest and torture of those who opposed the Communist party—led Boleslaw Walesa's youngest son, Lech, into a different field of work. As the founder

of Solidarity—the first legal, independent trade union in a Soviet-ruled country—Walesa dared to risk his own life so that the Polish people might at last live and work in peace.

Lech Walesa does not dwell on past mistakes. "I'm more interested in facing a new day than in looking backwards," he wrote in his autobiography, *A Way of Hope.* Yet at the same time he reminds us that past crimes must never be forgotten and that the struggle for human rights still goes on: "In Poland today, anti-Semitism is no longer the issue it once was, but that doesn't mean we can overlook the major part it played in our past. Even if it seems to have little bearing on current events, we are duty-bound to bear witness to the fate of those who, especially under the Nazis, were no longer even fighting for their lives, but merely for a dignified death."

The Poles had never known a leader like Lech Walesa. He was neither a king nor a dictator nor a puppet of a foreign country. His fellow Poles call him their "beloved president." But in his own words, he is simply "a man of the soil."

Lech Walesa waves to the crowd after successfully negotiating an end to the shipyard workers' strike in 1980.

The Walesa Family

At the end of the 18th century, Lech Walesa's ancestors settled in the little village of Popowo in north-central Poland. The name Walesa means "he who roams," and Lech's grandfather, Jan Walesa, lived up to his name. He spent most of his life going back and forth between France and Poland. But eventually he ran out of money and had to sell most of the land he had inherited from his father.

To his grandchildren, "Grandfather Jan" was the best storyteller in the world. "No one could halt the flow of reminiscences about his escapades in the towns of western Europe," Lech notes in his autobiography. Jan was full of life and full of fun, he wrote. But a contemporary of Jan's also described him in this way: "[He was] always trying to sell something in order to make some money. It went through his fingers like water, and his own children lacked the basic essentials. His sons didn't take after their father. [They] worked on the neighboring estates building houses and sheds for the animals."

When Grandfather Jan died, there were only a few acres of land left in Popowo to be divided among his 24 heirs—including Boleslaw Walesa, Lech Walesa's father.

Lech Walesa attends a mass with his son Slawek and his wife, Danuta.

Boleslaw made the most of his small farm, but after marrying Feliksa Kaminska, he knew more money would be needed to raise a family. Income from building houses and sheds helped to make ends meet. Boleslaw's brother Stanislaw joined him in the construction business, and Feliksa and Boleslaw named their second son, Stanislaw, after him. Their fourth child, Lech, was born on September 29, 1943, during Hitler's reign of terror in Poland.

When Boleslaw's brother escaped from one of Hitler's labor camps, Boleslaw refused to tell the Nazis where he was hiding (in a nearby forest). Because of his refusal to cooperate with the Nazis, Boleslaw was forced into a labor camp, too. The hard labor, beatings, bad food, and terrible conditions (only thin sheets were provided in below-zero weather), ruined Boleslaw's health. Lech was only one year old when his father came home to die in 1945. His last wish was for his brother Stanislaw to raise his children, and in 1946 Feliksa and Stanislaw were married.

Lech grew up with full knowledge of the horror Hitler had inflicted upon the Polish people. He knew why his father had died: to protect his brother's safety in the forest, a hiding place for the brave citizen-soldiers of Poland's Home Army who did their best to resist Nazi terrorism.

Feliksa raised her children to be honest, religious, and informed about Polish history (she was an ardent reader herself), and the Walesas walked together regularly to church two miles away. But the children—Izabela, Edward, Stanislaw, and Lech—never warmed up to their

Maria Victoria Walesa whispers in her father's ear during an outdoor mass in Gdansk.

stepfather. He was strict and often argued strongly with their mother—too strongly, as far as Lech was concerned. At times Lech would interrupt his mother and stepfather and plead for a peaceful solution to their disputes. He would ask them both to "sit down, think carefully and . . . explain your arguments without getting worked up." And as he explained in his autobiography, "I loved my mother dearly and was fiercely defensive of her." It seems that Lech learned early to value thoughtful negotiation as the way to bring peace.

Lech's school was run by the church until it was taken over by the Soviet-controlled Communist party in 1952. Communist history lessons left out much of the truth about Poland—its brave Home Army, the union formed by Hitler and Stalin, the suppression of human rights under both dictators, and other facts. But Lech knew the truth and dared to correct the teachers at every chance. Later he became even more outspoken in his pursuit of the truth.

Life at home for the Walesa children—including three half brothers—was also challenging, as Lech described in *A Way of Hope*:

Lech Walesa's sons during a visit to the tomb of the Unknown Soldier during a 1982 trip to Warsaw while their father remained jailed for his political activities.

23

Even the youngest had his or her own jobs to do: There were too many mouths to feed to allow for idlers. At the age of five we tended geese, at seven we took the cows out to pasture, at ten we took care of the other animals and did a variety of manual jobs—all that on top of school. The craftiest children pretended to be unusually interested in learning some subject or other if they wanted to avoid a particularly difficult or unpleasant task.

But Lech and his friends had fun too. "In summer," he wrote, "we used to rush to the edge of the lake, fling ourselves into the water and swim out as far as possible . . . or we played soccer with a ball made of rags or stuffed with horsehair." In winter they would straddle the cracking ice on the pond, jumping from one piece to another. "It was a test of courage," Lech wrote. "The one who went out the farthest . . . was the winner. In this kind of competition I frequently outdid my school fellows, but not in much else."

Though Lech was qualified to enter the College of Technology (he excelled in math and physics), his parents

Lech Walesa takes a break from politics to enjoy a day of fishing in a lake near his home.

could not afford to send him there. So in 1959 Lech decided to leave home for vocational school in Lipno, where he claimed a "young good-for-nothing like me" would be trained for work in industry. (He had made up his mind that farm work was not for him. "You never knew," he wrote, "whether something would grow or whether it would be eaten up by insects or pecked up by birds.")

Lech hoped to become an engineer someday, but little did he realize that from Lipno he would take giant steps in his profession and end up in the highest office in the land!

The Troublemaker

At vocational school in Lipno, Lech was called "a bit of a bully but a likeable one." He had a stocky build, a lot of energy, and "an absence of fear," as Mary Craig described in *Lech Walesa and His Poland*. And like Grandfather

Jan, he loved to laugh and enjoyed practical jokes. But it was his ability to organize that impressed his co-workers and superiors. The school's current director called it "an amazing gift." Given a task, Lech would do it quickly and thoroughly, delegating jobs in a highly professional manner. At the same time, he earned the label "troublemaker" for being outspoken and for breaking rules about smoking. (He and his friends would often smoke on the roof, where they couldn't be seen.) Though he received only fair grades at Lipno, Lech was reported "sound in morals and politics."

After graduation in 1961, he took a job as an electrician in the State Agricultural Department, and in 1963 was drafted into the Polish army. It was in the army that Lech grew his bushy mustache, which became his trademark. Though Polish soldiers were indoctrinated into Soviet-style communism, Lech and other Poles had learned long ago the value of religious faith and basic rights of individuals. Immunized against propaganda by his loving mother and family in Popowo, Lech was never fooled by the atheistic and dictatorial dogma hurled at him in the army. Lech laughed off much of what

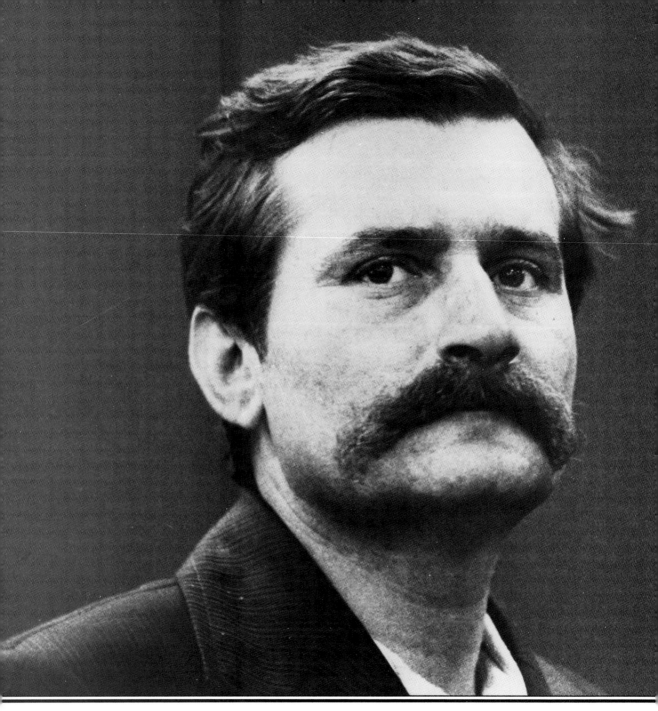

Lech Walesa as the spokesman for the striking Lenin Shipyard workers.

he heard, and his humor was contagious. His fellow servicemen liked to kid him, as Mary Craig recounts in one of their tales: "I remember him [Lech] coming to the cookhouse and asking, 'What's cooking?' And we all shouted back: 'Walesa's whiskers.'"

When his superiors offered Lech a chance to go to officers' training school, Lech turned it down, choosing to stay a part of the working class he was used to. So, after the army, Lech returned to his job as an electrician at the State Agriculture Department. He soon earned the nickname Golden Hands because of his ability to fix anything in sight. And he became extremely popular among his peers.

But at the age of 24, Lech felt he was no longer growing in his job; he was restless and wanted to move on. Also, he and a girlfriend had ended their relationship: "The girl sensibly made the decision for both of us and broke it off," he recalls in his autobiography. "I wasn't really sad, but I felt lonely and empty . . . it was a hard blow to my pride. Hence, my decision to leave and get away from home. . . . I needed a change of air . . . a big town, a port, adventure."

Stopover in Gdansk

In May 1967, seeking adventure and a better job, Lech boarded a train for Gdynia on the Baltic Sea. The train made a short stop in Gdansk, where Lech got off until the train was ready to leave. But he lingered too long in the station, and the train left for Gdynia without him.

As he walked outside the station, he met an old friend from Lipno, who encouraged him to stay in Gdansk and work for the Lenin Shipyard. Lech took the advice, applied for a job, and got one. He knew that Poland was famous for its quality ships, and he was proud to be a part of his country's important industry—particularly at the Lenin Shipyard, whose products were considered excellent examples of modern shipbuilding.

But soon he found out that working conditions were horrible: Employees often worked ten hours a day for the lowest wages. At first he worked as an electrician who laid cables on fishing boats, and was just one of 15,000 workers. His goal was to become an electromechanic.

Lech lived with the Krol family and enjoyed listening to Radio Free Europe and discussing politics with Mr. Krol. But soon the working conditions, long hours, and low wages began to affect Walesa, leaving him little time

Lech Walesa speaks to reporters covering the workers' strike at the Lenin Shipyard.

off for fun. However, a stop in a flower shop one day in May 1968 lightened up his life considerably.

While stopping at the little shop to get some change, he was struck by the beauty and kind manner of the shop's cashier—a woman named Danuta Golos. He later returned to ask her for a date, and soon the couple fell in love. Both had grown up on farms, surrounded by large families, and both had decided to leave the country life for adventure in the city. The more they knew about each other, the more they wanted to share life together. And on November 8, 1969, Lech and Danuta were married.

They began married life in an attic above a beauty shop, and in light of the shortage of affordable housing for Polish workers, they felt lucky to find a place at all. Soon their first child, Bogdan ("gift of God"), was born, and Lech realized that he would have to work harder than ever as his family began to grow.

Walesa was well liked among his fellow workers at the shipyard, and because of his leadership ability and organizational skills, he soon became a job inspector. As inspector he learned more about the employees and the conditions they worked under. The workers trusted him

Lech Walesa thanks Danuta for all of her support during his political activities.

and felt free to tell him their complaints without being punished. Lech Walesa was their friend . . . and would soon become their leader.

In 1968, after the government banned the performance of a play because it was "anti-Russian," students protested the lack of free speech and free press and staged an open demonstration in the streets of Warsaw. The Catholic church, headed by Cardinal Stefan Wyszynski, rallied to the students' cause. Walesa urged workers to support the students, but the government persuaded most of the workers to oppose the protest. The students failed to win the workers' support, but the experience ignited Walesa's passion to win freedom for the Polish people. He knew there was much work to be done to right the wrongs that were spreading in the workplace.

It was difficult to form "bonds of solidarity" at the shipyard, as he explained in his autobiography.

At the yard . . . each of us was just a tiny cog in a vast machine. Although we did represent a certain collective strength that had to be taken

Workers striking for better wages and working conditions listen to the
words of their leader, Lech Walesa.

into account when things weren't going well—and they rarely did—we worked in an atmosphere of unrelieved tension and gloom. The men were dressed alike, in shabby attire, and we seemed to behave in a vaguely military fashion, almost by reflex. . . . The fact was we were shuffled about in a way which left us with little control over our destinies.

But it was not long before Walesa and his co-workers dared to take control of their lives. On December 12, 1970, the government doubled food prices throughout Poland—in time to ruin the holiday season for workers and their families. More than 9,000 workers marched in protest, and Lech Walesa was one of their leaders.

Walesa hoped the demonstration would be non-violent, but the government turned it into a riot when its soldiers fired on the workers, killing four of Walesa's friends. From then on he was more determined than ever to bring justice to his country, and the workers looked to him as their leader, the chief champion of their cause. The government recognized Walesa's popularity and his remarkable power as an organizer, and even tried to lure him into informing on his fellow workers!

In 1973, as life in Poland became more difficult, Walesa's mother and stepfather decided to leave their small farm, where they faced starvation, and move to the United States. They hoped to find financial security there and planned to return to Poland a few years later. But in 1975 Lech's mother was killed in a traffic accident. The loss deeply saddened Lech, but also made him even more anxious to push forward in his fight for human rights and fair prices and wages in Poland, as his mother would have wanted him to.

Walesa continued to fight the oppressive conditions at the shipyard, and after another public demonstration in 1976, he was finally fired. The label "troublemaker" followed him wherever he went, because he was never afraid to speak the truth . . . even when it contradicted the government's views. His efforts were echoed by the KOR, the Committee for the Defense of Workers, begun by Polish intellectuals who shared Walesa's goal—to protect the rights of workers.

Walesa moved from one job to another trying to

support his growing family, which finally included eight children. And Danuta provided the strength and support Walesa needed for the struggle ahead.

Danuta

"I owe many of my most important decisions to her," Lech Walesa wrote about his wife, Danuta. "Not that she ever told me what to do exactly; she simply talked to me in a way that helped me to see things from a new angle."

Danuta and Lech shared household duties as well as political activities. "With Danuta, I've washed the babies' diapers, bathed and fed the children," he wrote. "There was simply too much to do to think of specifying what was a wife's and what was a husband's job. This physical contact with my children, from the earliest moments, has brought us close forever. . . ."

Danuta supported her husband's active role in the Free Trade Unions Movement, which, like all groups that

Danuta and Lech Walesa relax in their small apartment.

Lech Walesa kisses the hand of a supporter while visiting the workshop where he had worked as an electrician.

opposed the government's violations of employees' rights, operated underground. She recognized her husband's charisma, which always attracted huge crowds wherever he appeared, and she listened carefully to all his speeches.

In *Lech Walesa and His Poland* Mary Craig describes the Walesa magic: "Lech Walesa had true charisma . . . he used words honestly. . . . Speaking the truth, even though his Polish was rough . . . [he] was offering the moral leadership for which Poland hungered."

By July 1980, under Communist party leader Edward Gierek, unrest was rampant in Poland. Meat shortages and rising food prices began to plague the people, as they had ten years earlier. Intellectuals and other activists were imprisoned for voicing their views about free speech, free press, and free trade unions.

But it was the firing of Anna Walentynowicz, a loyal shipyard worker, honored for the quality of her work, that enraged her co-workers and helped spark the famous strike of 1980. Why was such an excellent worker fired? Anna had fought against injustice and had spoken out in the *Coastal Worker*, a popular paper among Polish workers, who were now ready to strike on her behalf and for all she represented—freedom and dignity in the workplace. Lech Walesa, then unemployed, returned to the shipyard to lead the strike.

With the power of the workers behind him, Walesa was confident he could not fail to achieve his goal. Supported by the intellectuals and Catholic activist Father Henryk Jankowski, his message now reached beyond Gdansk to unhappy Poles throughout the country.

Finally, as depicted in the famous photo that appeared on front pages around the world, Lech Walesa, surrounded by thousands of cheering workers, jumped on top of a bulldozer at the shipyard and called for the strike to begin. Their basic rights must no longer be denied, he said. And they won.

As a result of the strike, workers were guaranteed higher wages, Walesa's job at the shipyard was restored, and Anna Walentynowicz was welcomed back as well. The agreements were carefully and skillfully worked out by Walesa and the government. But Walesa called an end to the strike only after the rights of *all* striking workers in Poland—not just in Gdansk—were granted. The

Lech Walesa greets cheering supporters at a special workers' mass in 1988.

agreements were signed on August 29, 1980. Using a pen decorated with a picture of Pope John Paul II, Lech Walesa signed his name.

It was a crucial victory for Walesa and the Polish people, and it gave his labor movement—Solidarity—new international prestige and power. Danuta was both excited and afraid about her husband's success, as she recalled in *A Way of Hope*: "I knew life would be different from then on, unknown territory stretched ahead of us both. Would it be for better or for worse?"

Solidarity

When the shipyard's director called out, "Strike in solidarity," the expression impressed Walesa and the other workers in Gdansk. They wanted to unite with the other, smaller groups that were also struggling for fair wages and the right to form their own labor organizations

Lech Walesa leads a march of Solidarity members in support of striking workers.

independent of government or management. When the strike in Gdansk became a strike in solidarity (unity) with the smaller, powerless groups in Poland, the name Solidarity was chosen for Walesa's movement, which included more than ten million Poles.

Though his bushy mustache and baggy pants made Walesa look every bit like an ordinary worker, he was courted by world leaders and the media from around the world. People loved him; he always spoke from the heart, with their best interests in mind. At the same time, he warned Poles about not going out on a limb by making unreasonable demands. Like Gandhi before him, Walesa wanted "to change people's way of thinking rather than to overthrow existing institutions," as he wrote in his autobiography. "We're in the process of working out a Polish style of socialism. We're asking the authorities to serve, not to lead. What happens in our country should be our affair."

Always the negotiator, Walesa tried to avoid the rise of radical factions within his organization. But in December 1981 the radical element caught Walesa off-guard by calling for a national vote to question the continuance of the Communist party in Poland. General

Wojciech Jaruzelski, Poland's prime minister and Communist party head, reacted quickly and violently. He trashed Solidarity's offices, made the organization illegal, arrested Walesa and other leaders, and declared martial law (military rule).

Tanks rolled through the streets, and citizens—including children—were arrested and beaten. Miners were murdered in Silesia because they tried to defend their free trade union. Others endured terrifying prison conditions. "It was my faith, together with an unshakable belief that Solidarity would win out in the end, that helped me through this period," Walesa wrote. Food, clothing, and fuel began to run out, and some people had to stand in line for 17 hours to buy enough food for one meal!

Letters from Pope John Paul II, a native of Poland, supporting Walesa's plea for peaceful talks to restore freedom to Poland, were sent directly to General Jaruzelski. On December 18, 1981, the pope wrote the following:

> During the last two centuries, the Polish nation has endured great wrongs, and much blood has been spilled in the struggle for power over our

Pope John Paul II holds the hands of Lech and Danuta Walesa during a private meeting.

Fatherland. Our history cries out against more bloodshed, and we must not allow this tragedy to continue to weigh so heavily on the conscience of the nation. I therefore appeal to you, General, to return to the methods of peaceful dialogue that have characterized efforts at social renewal since August 1980. . . . The welfare of the entire nation depends on it. People throughout the world, all those who rightly see the cause of peace furthered by respect for the rights of Man, are waiting for this return to nonviolent means. All humanity's desire for peace argues for an end to the state of martial law in Poland.

On November 15, 1982, after 11 months in jail, Walesa was freed, but was put under constant surveillance by the government. Solidarity continued to operate underground. Radio equipment and printing supplies were sneaked into Poland from the United States and other democratic countries so that Solidarity's message—"Solidarity lives!"—would continue to be heard and newsletters like *Solidarity Weekly* could still be published. In the United States people showed support for Walesa by organizing marches in solidarity with his courageous efforts.

And in 1983 workers in Gdansk and all over Poland rejoiced when Lech Walesa was awarded the prestigious Nobel Peace Prize.

The Prize and the Presidency

Lech Walesa was both surprised and thrilled to win the honored Nobel Prize. He described the day the news was announced in Gdansk: "People were shouting: Lech! Lech! Walesa! Walesa! and Solidarity! Solidarity! There were flowers, happy faces and lots of friends, all of them invigorated by the news." And he told the crowd: "I see this as a prize for us all, as a reward to each of us who wished to attain the truth by following the cause of nonviolence and common understanding."

Lech Walesa waves to the crowd after learning of his Nobel Prize win.

Walesa announced that the money he received from the Nobel Peace Prize would go to the Agricultural Development Fund because "we all have to eat," he said. And he asked Danuta to accept the award for him at the ceremony in Oslo, Norway, because he was afraid that once he left Poland he would not be allowed back into his own country.

Danuta felt honored to represent her husband at the ceremony in Oslo on December 10, 1983. Walesa listened to her read his acceptance speech on the radio with his friend Father Jankowski and others in Gdansk. Thanks to Radio Free Europe, Poles were able to hear the memorable speech:

> You are aware of the reasons why I could not come to your capital city and receive personally this distinguished prize. On that solemn day my place is among those with whom I have grown and to whom I belong—the workers of Gdansk.
>
> Let my words convey to you the joy and the never-extinguished hope of the millions of my brothers—the millions of working people in

factories and offices, associated in the union whose very name expresses one of the noblest aspirations of humanity. Today all of them, like myself, feel greatly honored by the Prize.

With deep sorrow I think of those who paid with their lives for their loyalty to Solidarity, of those who are behind prison bars and who are victims of repression. I think of all those with whom I have traveled the same road and with whom I share the trials and tribulations of our time.

For the first time a Pole has been awarded a prize which Alfred Nobel founded for activities toward bringing the nations of the world closer together.

The most ardent hopes of my compatriots are linked with this idea—in spite of the violence, cruelty and brutality which characterizes the conflicts splitting the present-day world.

We desire peace, and that is why we have never resorted to physical force. We crave for justice, and that is why we are so persistent in the struggle for our rights. We seek freedom of convictions, and that is why we have never attempted to enslave man's conscience nor shall we ever attempt to do so.

We are fighting for the right of the working people to organize and for the dignity of human labor. We respect the dignity and the rights of every man and every nation. The road to a brighter future for the world leads through honest reconciliation of conflicting interests and not through hatred and bloodshed. To follow that road means to enhance the moral power of the all-embracing idea of human solidarity.

May I express to you, the distinguished representatives of the Norwegian people, my most profound gratitude for confirming the vitality and strength of our ideas by awarding the Nobel Prize to the chairman of Solidarity.

"I was overcome with emotion," he wrote. "My heart melted when I heard Danuta's voice coming to me from so far away. . . . I can still remember the music that was playing, and the joyful melodious voice of the journalist commenting on the atmosphere of the Nobel ceremony. It was one of the most beautiful moments of my life."

Martial law finally ended in Poland, but it was followed by years of economic and political problems—and more strikes by the workers. In spite of his international reputation, Walesa claimed, "I am just an ordinary worker." He worked day and night to keep Solidarity alive. And when Soviet president Mikhail Gorbachev visited Poland in 1988, he realized—and warned—that the Polish Communist government could not govern without the support of Solidarity.

Finally, the troubled Polish Communist rulers seemed to have nowhere to turn but to the one man who had the organizational skills and quality of leadership needed to solve Poland's problems—their foe, Lech Walesa. And in 1989 the government went to him for advice. After many meetings with Walesa, the master negotiator, Solidarity was legalized, and open elections were allowed. And for the first time in a Soviet-controlled country, elections included non-Communists.

On December 9, 1990, Lech Walesa was elected president of Poland. Solidarity was born again, and

workers all over the country cheered for their friend. Never before had they witnessed one of their own—a hardworking engineer from a humble background— achieve such stature. The election gave them hope that human rights in Poland would become a reality at last.

When reporters asked Walesa about the secrets to his success and his theories on politics and economics, he gave a typical, honest response, as expressed in *A Way of Hope*:

> I do my best to look on political events in the same light as my personal problems, and try to resolve them similarly. I never take a tragic view of life. Even if nothing in this world really depends on us, that shouldn't excuse us from putting all our efforts, in a dignified way, into finding the best possible solutions, and the most honest ones. I've met too many embittered people, politicians especially, who'd been forced out of office and were obsessed with one overriding idea—their own—beside which nothing else counted, nothing else even existed. This is why I always find it

Lech and Bogden Walesa cast their votes during the first parliamentary election featuring a Solidarity candidate.

difficult when people ask me what my theory is: what theory I identify with totally. To tell the truth, I don't identify myself with a theory at all. Not because I'm a skeptic, but because I'm a man of the soil, not the academy.

Road to Recovery

Since Walesa's election to the presidency, Poland has become a model for other Eastern European countries that are changing from communism to democratic forms of government. But, as Walesa told the news media in 1992, any dramatic change in government "brings chaos at first." Unemployment is a natural result when state-owned businesses close down. But as private enterprises begin to grow, problems will be solved.

Already, unemployment in Gdansk—today, one of Europe's richest port cities—is stabilizing, Walesa said, but workers' salaries are still too low and in need of

Former U.S. president George Bush bestows the Medal of Freedom to Lech Walesa during a 1989 visit to the White House.

Seated in front of a Solidarity banner, Lech Walesa listens to the demands of a farmers' union.

guarantees for the future. Negotiation is needed between the existing parties in Poland to bring lasting unity. In order to bring about the necessary changes in his country, Walesa wants to make sure that his role as president is not just a ceremonial one; he believes a new constitution should be approved by the new democratically elected Parliament so that he will have the authority to make the changes the people elected him to make. The Communist-based constitution, they believe, is a thing of the past. "We are making an historic transition," Walesa said on international television, "and I would fight to my death any move to go back to the old form of government, to the loss of freedom."

Perhaps President Walesa's vision is summed up best in the final words of his autobiography: "There will come a time, which I won't live to see, when narrow Polish problems have been brushed aside, replaced by harmony and peace over our entire planet. . . . Until that time we have work to do."

For Further Reading

Brolewicz, Walter. *My Brother Lech Walesa*. New York: Tribeca Communications, Inc., 1983.

Craig, Mary. *Lech Walesa and His Poland*. New York: The Continuum Publishing Company, 1987.

Jampolsky, Gerald. *One Person Can Make a Difference*. New York: Bantam Books, 1990.

Kaye, Tony. *Lech Walesa*. New York: Chelsea House Publishers, 1989.

Walesa, Lech. *A Way of Hope*. New York: Henry Holt and Company, 1987.

Index

About the Author

Caroline Evensen Lazo was born in Minneapolis, Minnesota. She spent much of her childhood visiting museums and attending plays written by her mother, Isobel Evensen, whose work earned national acclaim and became a lasting source of inspiration for her daughter.

Ms. Lazo attended the University of Oslo, Norway, and received a B.A. in Art History from the University of Minnesota. She has written extensively about art and architecture, and is the author of many books for young people, including *The Terra Cotta Army of Emperor Qin*, *Missing Treasure*, and *Endangered Species*.